The Optical Illusion Book

THE OPTICAL ILLUSION BOOK

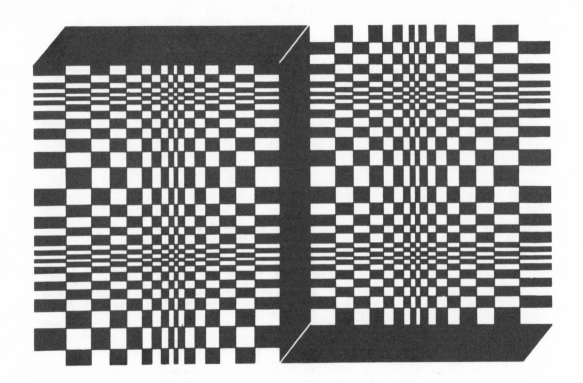

BY SEYMOUR SIMON

Drawings by Constance Ftera

William Morrow and Company • New York • 1984

FOR JOYCE WITH LOVE

10 9 8 7

Library of Congress Cataloging in Publication Data
Simon, Seymour. The optical illusion book.
Includes index. Summary: A discussion of optical illusions with
explanations of why we see them and suggestions for creating illusions
of our own. 1. Optical illusions—Juvenile literature. [1. Optical
illusions] I. Ftera, Constance, ill. II. Title.
QP495.S57   1984   152.1'48   83-43222
ISBN 0-688-03255-9 (lib. bdg.)
ISBN 0-688-03254-0 (pbk.)

CONTENTS

The Optical Illusion Book

Do you believe everything you see? Are you sure? Look at the two straight lines in Figure A-1. Which is longer, line AB or line CD?

It certainly looks as though line CD is longer. But is it really? You'll need a ruler to tell for sure. Measure each line. Both lines are the same length, even though one *looks* longer.

Another example is Figure A-2. Which line is longer, AB or BC? Again, the line that looks longer may not really be longer. Measure each line with your ruler. Surprised at the result? Both lines are exactly the same length.

You have been looking at two optical or visual illusions. An optical illusion is something you see that is not exactly what is really there. You see one line to be longer than another, even though both really are the same size.

There are many different kinds of optical illusions. Some you see each day in nature, such as the way the sun or moon appears to move when clouds float by. Other illusions are done purposefully to fool you, such as the way artists make you see distance in a flat drawing.

INTRODUCTION:
Seeing Is Believing

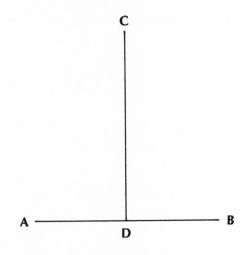

Figure A–1

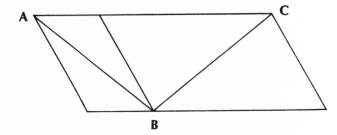

Figure A–2

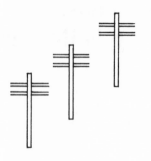

Figure A–3

Look at the three telegraph poles in Figure A-3.

When you see them without any background, they are the same size. But look what happens when you place a few simple lines in the background in Figure A-4.

Now which telegraph pole looks bigger? To make them appear to be the same size, the artist would deliberately make each pole a different size. In so doing, the artist makes an illusion of distance in a picture that is really flat, like in Figure A-5.

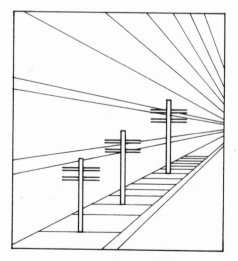

Figure A–4

Figure A–5

We are going to show you many optical illusions in this book. We'll also try to explain why you see them the way you do. Show some of them to your friends. It's fun to share in the illusion of seeing and not believing.

Just to show you that everything may not be so simple to figure out, try looking at Figure A-6. Can you see where the three prongs come from? Try drawing the figure on another sheet of paper. Even if you can draw it, you may not believe it!

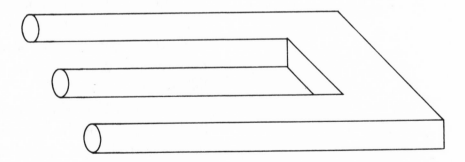

Figure A–6

How You See

It is not just your eyes that let you see. You see because of the cooperation of nerve cells in your eyes, with nerve cells in your brain, and the connection between them called the optic nerve.

Your eye is shaped like a small ball about one inch across. It sits in a cuplike socket in the front of your head. Your eyelids hide part of your eye and make it appear oval-shaped. Four sets of small muscles hold your eyeball in its socket. The muscles make your eye move side to side and up and down.

A cross section of your eye looks something like Figure 1-1. The *cornea* is a clear, protective covering. It lets in light, but keeps out dust and other harmful things. Just behind the cornea is the *lens*. The lens focuses the light coming into your eye. The light forms an image which falls on the *retina*.

The amount of light coming into your eye is regulated by the *iris*. This is the colored part of your eye. The iris opens and closes depending on the brightness of the light. The black dot in the center of the iris is where the light enters. It is called the *pupil*.

Here is what happens when you look at something, say a pencil in your hand. Light reflected from the pencil and your hand enters your eye through your pupil. The lens forms the light into an image that is a small picture of the pencil in your hand. The image falls upside down on the retina.

The retina contains more than one hundred million sensitive nerve cells. There are two kinds of nerve cells in the retina: *rods* and *cones*. (We'll tell you more about them in the chapter on color, page 49.) When light strikes the retina, the nerve cells respond. They send out tiny electric currents called nerve impulses.

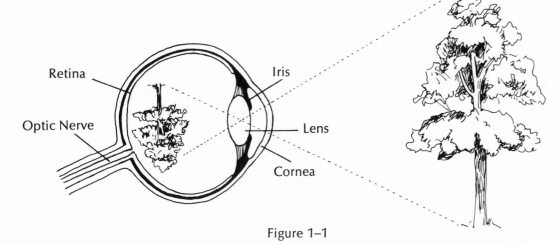

Figure 1–1

The impulses travel along the cells to the optic nerve. The nerve cells that make up the optic nerve carry the impulses to the cells in the brain.

It is in your mind that the act of seeing finally takes place. Your brain puts together the nerve impulses from your eyes along with impulses from other cells of your brain. All these interacting impulses become the picture that you see.

Of course, we don't know exactly how the brain works. We are not sure how patterns of nerve impulses are created and why they remain or change. We don't know where the brain stores its previous information. But scientists are now working on many of these questions. Perhaps we will soon begin to learn some of the answers. And no doubt, the answers will, in turn, lead to new questions.

Some interesting experiments already have been done on the nature of seeing. For example, we know that an electric shock or a blow to certain parts of your head can cause you to see lights. *(Don't try it. It may cause severe injury.)* This goes along with the expression that a person "sees stars" when hit on the head. The cells on the retina will release nerve impulses just as if they had been stimulated by light rays.

By the way, there is one spot on the retina that is not sensitive to light. It has no rods or cones. It is called the *blind spot.* It is located at the point where the optic nerve enters the retina. Each of your eyes has a blind spot.

Normally, you are not aware of the blind spots. Your eyes are constantly shifting around. They will provide you with enough information about the scene you see so that you will not notice the blind spot.

But there is an easy way to become aware of the blind spot in your eye. Look at Figure 1-2. Close your left eye. Hold the book at arm's length and look straight at the X with your right eye. Keep staring straight at the X while you slowly bring the book closer to your eye. At some point, about six to ten inches from your eye, you will no longer see the dot. If you bring the book closer, the

X

Figure 1–2

dot will appear again. At the point that you can't see the dot, the light from it falls just on the blind spot.

If you want to check the blind spot in your left eye, turn the book over. Now close your right eye. Stare directly at the X with your left eye and follow directions as above.

In the next chapter we will look at some of the ways that your eyes and your brain can sometimes come to a mistaken conclusion about what you are seeing.

Finding out why you see an optical illusion may not be very easy. For example, Figure 2-1 is the first optical illusion shown in the introduction to this book.

You already know that both lines are the same length, even though line CD looks longer. Try showing this illusion to your friends or classmates. Almost all of them probably will see line CD as the longer one.

A number of years ago, the illusion was explained in this way. The theory stated it is more difficult to raise your eyes upward a certain distance than to move them sideward the same distance. But this explanation doesn't hold up when we investigate more carefully. For one thing, it hasn't been proven that it's more difficult to move your eyes upward. Furthermore, no one has shown that the difficulty would make the line seem longer.

But perhaps you can best prove that the theory is wrong by yourself. Draw the figure sideways, like in Figure 2-2.

Which line looks longer now? Ask your friends. Most people think that CD still looks longer. But line CD is now sideward. So the explanation about the difficulty in

Why You See Optical Illusions

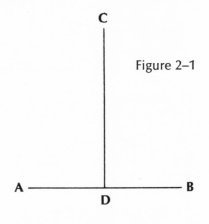

Figure 2–1

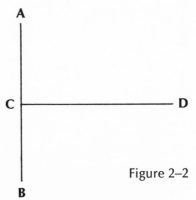

Figure 2–2

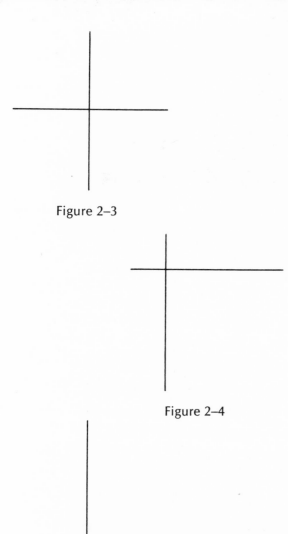

Figure 2–3

Figure 2–4

Figure 2–5

moving your eyes upward and sideward doesn't seem to work.

Another explanation for this illusion seems to hold up better. The reason that line AB seems shorter is because line CD interrupts it. For example, most people see no illusion if the lines interrupt each other equally as in Figure 2-3 and Figure 2-4.

But if the lines interrupt each other at different points, the illusion comes back as in Figure 2-5 and Figure 2-6.

So perhaps this newer theory is the correct one. But we can't be sure. In science, we believe a theory only as long as it helps us to explain the evidence. If new evidence comes up that the theory cannot explain, then we must develop a new theory.

Figure 2-7 and Figure 2-8 are two more illusions. The two horizontal lines are equal in length in both drawings, even though the top ones look longer.

The theory about what makes this illusion work goes by the name of *perspective.* If you look down a highway or a railway line, the sides of the road or the line seem to come together in the distance. An artist uses this idea when he wants us to see depth in a scene he's drawing on a flat surface.

Try these illusions on your friends. Most of us have seen lines like this so often in drawings and also in photographs, that we accept the narrowing part as being farther away. Even though your eye sees the two horizontal lines as equal in length, your brain uses other information to interpret what you see.

Using previous experience with perspective, your brain decides that the top line is farther away than the bottom line. It then concludes that a farther object that appears to be the same size as a closer object, must actually be larger. Of course, you are not conscious of this process in your brain. You only are aware of the result. To you, the top line just looks longer.

Even though all your friends see the same illusion, not everybody in the world is fooled. You might guess that people who have no experience with perspective in drawings or photographs would not see this illusion.

Some scientists tried out these illusions on some people in an African country called Uganda. The Ugandans

Figure 2–6

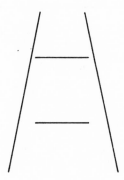

Figure 2–7

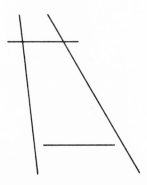

Figure 2–8

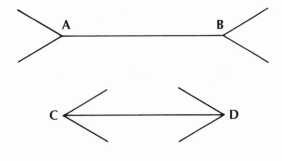

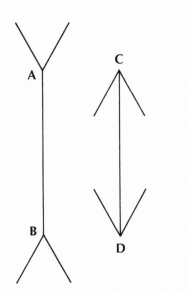

Figure 2–9

Figure 2–10

who lived in cities and had experience with drawings and photographs were fooled by the illusion. The Ugandans who lived in the back country and had never seen perspective drawings or photographs were not fooled. They saw both lines as being equal in length.

You can understand that it is not just your eyes that see an optical illusion. The way you see things has a lot to do with your previous experience. That helps to explain why not everyone sees the same optical illusions.

This theory about the importance of previous experience can be supported by still another illusion. It is called the Muller-Lyer illusion, after the scientist who discovered it and is shown in Figure 2-9 and Figure 2-10.

Which lines look longer to you, AB or CD? Use a ruler to prove that both lines are really the same length. Ask your friends to look at these drawings. The chances are that all of them will think as you do. Line AB just seems longer than CD.

Does everyone around the world see this illusion? Again, scientists found that some people do not. Certain African tribespeople who had little contact with modern technology saw the illusion while other tribes did not. What could be the reason?

Here is the theory that seems to help explain. The Muller-Lyer drawings look to us something like the edges of buildings or boxes or other square objects. Look at Figure 2-11 for example.

We are used to seeing drawings of things in perspective. So a line (AB) that appears to be farther away and yet the same size as a closer line (CD) must actually be larger. That's why the Muller-Lyer illusion works for us.

Figure 2–11

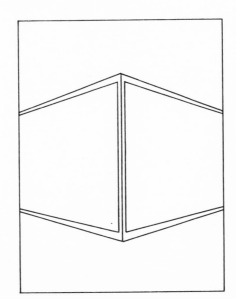
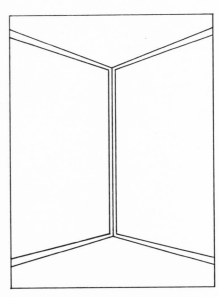

Some African tribes have round houses and doors with curved edges. They have no boxes and rarely see anything that has a right-angle edge. They also do not use perspective in their art and are not familiar with photographs. According to the theory, these facts help explain why they are not fooled by the Muller-Lyer illusion.

It seems more and more certain that this theory is correct. We see many illusions not because our eyes see them, but because our brain uses previous experiences to interpret what our eyes see.

One of the most interesting things about this optical illusion is that you can draw equal lines yourself, yet still see them as unequal. Start by drawing three horizontal lines, all the same length, as in Figure 3-1.

They look equal in size at this point. Now add vertical or slanting lines to the end of each line just as in Figure 3-2.

The added lines change the way we see three horizontal lines. The top line seems larger than the middle line and the middle line seems larger than the bottom line. This is so even though you know that you drew the lines to be equal in length.

The reason for this illusion again seems to deal with perspective. That is, the more the end lines slant, the farther away the horizontal lines seem to be. Because of this the top line seems farthest away. But the top horizontal line is the same size as the middle and the bottom line. So our brain concludes that a line farther away that appears to be the same size as a closer one, must really be longer.

You can destroy this illusion just by rearranging the order of the lines, as in Figure 3-3.

Lines and Spaces

Figure 3–1

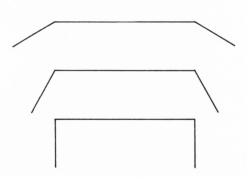

Figure 3–2

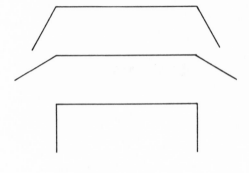

Figure 3–3

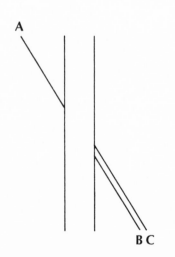

Figure 3–4

Now you no longer have any perspective in the drawing. One line doesn't seem any farther away than another line. So all the lines that are equal will look equal.

Sometimes you can consciously try and change the way an illusion looks to you. Look back at Figure 3-2. Try to pay no attention to the top line. Look at the middle and the bottom horizontal line. After awhile, you should be able to make them look equal.

Figure 3-4 is another drawing that you can consciously change if you study it.

Is line B or C a continuation of line A? At first line C looks like the continuation. But use a ruler or other straight edge and place it on the figure. You can see that line B is really the continuation of line A. Remove the ruler and you can probably force yourself to continue seeing the lines correctly. Still another way to see the figure correctly is to turn it until lines A, B, and C are horizontal. That destroys the illusion.

Here's another illusion that you can change by shifting your point of view. The long lines in Figure 3-5 look as if they slant toward each other. But hold the book up to your eye. Turn the book sideways and sight along the long lines. The short crossing lines are no longer easy to see. The long lines now look parallel to each other. Again perspective seems to play a part in Figure 3-5.

Here are some drawings that may not be so easy for you to see correctly no matter how you hold them. In Figure 3-6 the two circles are the same size.

Figure 3–5

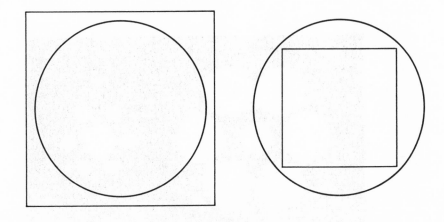

Figure 3–6

The two circles in Figure 3-7 are also the same size. They appear unequal because of their position in the angled lines.

Figure 3-8 has equal-sized circles that appear unequal because of the surrounding circles. The center circles are both the same size. The one on the right seems larger because we compare it to the surrounding smaller circles. The one on the left seems smaller because we compare it to the surrounding larger circles.

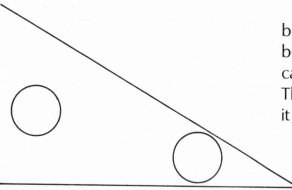

Figure 3–7

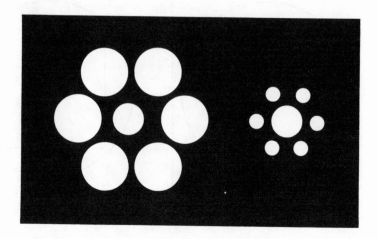

Figure 3–8

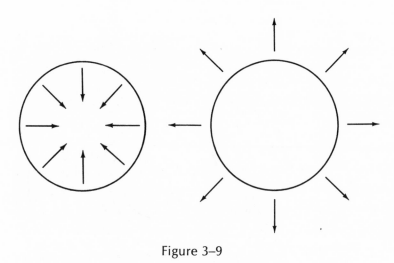

Figure 3–9

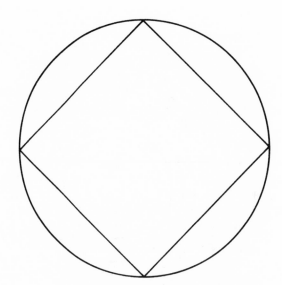

Figure 3–10

The two circles in Figure 3-9 are also equal in size. The arrows within circle A seem to pull it inward and make the circle appear smaller. The arrows outside circle B seem to pull outward and make the circle appear larger.

Sometimes a circle doesn't even seem like a circle because of its surroundings. In Figure 3-10, the circle appears to pull in at each point that it intersects the inside square.

In Figure 3-11, the circles appear distorted. The background pattern of slanting lines causes this effect.

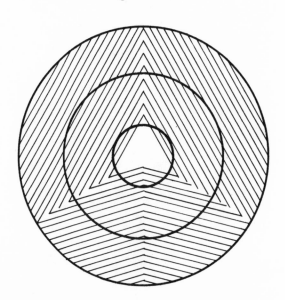

Figure 3–11

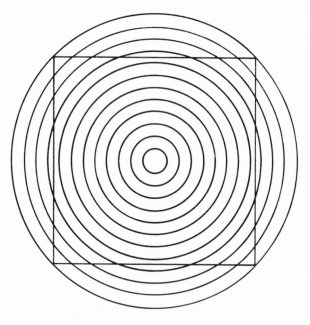

Figure 3–12

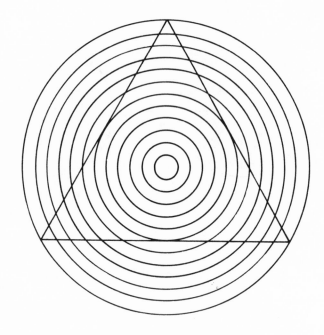

Figure 3–13

We can also use circles to make straight lines appear to bend. Figure 3-12 is really a square against a background of circles. The sides of the square appear to bend inward because of the pulling effect of the circles on our eyes.

The triangle in Figure 3-13 has straight-line sides. Again the circles make the lines appear to bend inward.

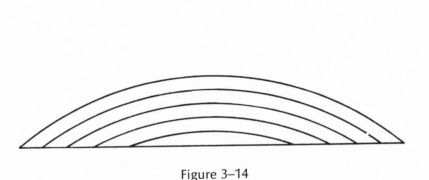

Figure 3–14

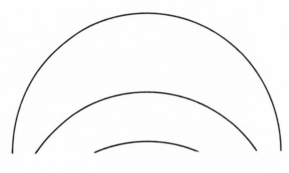

Figure 3–15

Even parts of a circle can make a straight line seem to bend. Look at Figure 3-14.

Sometimes parts of the same circle don't seem to have the same curve. Figure 3-15 shows three arcs of the same circle. The differences in their sizes appear to make each arc curve differently. Place the edge of a cut-out paper circle over each arc to show them to be alike.

Figure 3-16 shows some circles that look like spirals. To prove that they are circles, trace one of them out with a compass.

Figure 3–16

Just the direction in which we look at a drawing may make it appear different. The two squares in Figure 3-17 are the same size. The one on the left looks larger because we view it as a diamond when it is tilted.

There are many different ways that lines and spaces can be arranged to make you see illusions. In the next chapter we will show you some illusions that continue to change as you look at them.

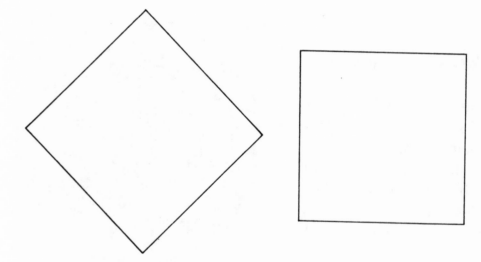

Figure 3–17

Here's an illusion that changes back and forth as you look at it. Is the bent card shown in Figure 4-1 facing toward you or away from you? You should be able to make it flip back and forth every few seconds.

The card seems to change easily because there is no reason to see it one way rather than another. Either way we see it makes equally good sense to us. Figure 4-2 is another drawing that we can see equally well in two different positions. It's called a reversing cube. Do you see the area bounded by the darker lines as the outside surface of a transparent box? Keep looking and the bounded area will become the inner surface of a box tilted in a different way. Now make it flip back and forth if you can.

Changeable Figures

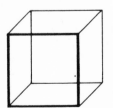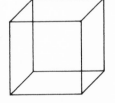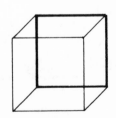

Figure 4–2

Figure 4–1

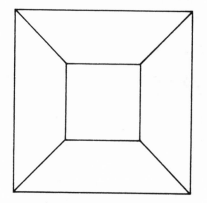

Figure 4–3

Does the center square of Figure 4-3 project toward you or away from you? Or does it do both?

Look at Figure 4-4. Which way does the staircase run? Keep looking and it will reverse in front of your eyes. If you don't see the reversal, think of one edge of a step as first nearer and then farther away.

Do the rings in Figure 4-5 show a hollow tube running from left to right or from right to left? Keep looking at the figure. Rapidly close and open each eye one at a time. What happens every time you blink an eye?

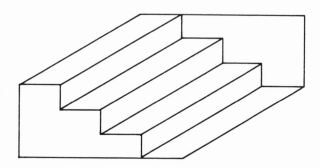

Figure 4–4

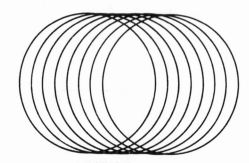

Figure 4–5

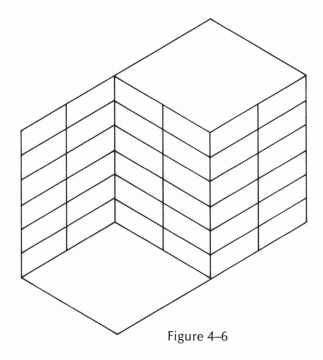

Figure 4–6

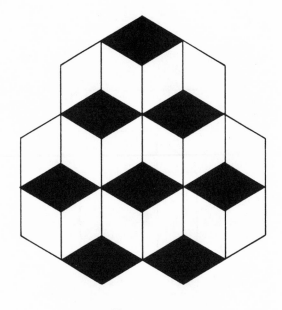

Figure 4–7

Do you see Figure 4-6 as a solid figure with one long edge, or do you see it as two solid figures leaning on each other? Keep looking to make it change from one to the other.

The drawing of boxes in Figure 4-7 may not seem to stay still long enough to be counted. Do you see six or seven stacked boxes? View the black diamonds as either the tops or the bottoms of the boxes.

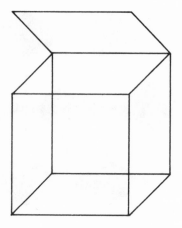

Figure 4–8

Figure 4-8 is a single box. The trouble with this box is that the lid is either open toward you or away from you. Which way do you see it? Keep looking to make it switch from one to the other.

Sometimes it's difficult to tell which is the object and which is the background. Look at Figure 4-9. Do you see this as white lines on a black background or black lines on a white background?

Figure 4–9

Figure 4–10

Figure 4–11

Which is the figure and which is the background in Figure 4-10? Do you see two faces staring at each other or a lovely vase?

At times we have to supply missing information in a drawing with our minds. Figure 4-11 is a bunch of oddly shaped black spots. Use your imagination to see a dog. (Would you call the dog "Spot"?)

Do you see anything in the black spots in Figure 4-12? Would you believe a horse and rider?

When a drawing becomes more complicated, it can cause us to see images which are really quite different from each other. For example, do you see a duck or a rabbit in Figure 4-13?

Figure 4–12

Do you see a pretty young girl or an old witch in Figure 4-14? (The young girl's chin becomes the witch's nose.)

Sometimes extra information in a drawing makes us see it one way or another. Figure 4-15 shows two sketches of a face. One seems to be looking straight at you, while the other seems to be looking over your shoulder. But cover the bottom halves of both faces. Keep looking at both pairs of the eyes. By making an effort, you can make both pairs of eyes seem to look directly at you. When you uncover the bottom of the drawing, the eyes of the figure on the left shift back.

Figure 4–13

Figure 4–15

Figure 4–14

Figure 4–16

In Figure 4-16, do you see black arrows pointing left and right? Or do you see white arrows pointing up and down?

Figure 4-17 shows some groups of dots. In the first group, the dots seem to be arranged in columns. In the second group, the dots seem to be arranged in lines. In the third group, you can see the dots as either columns or lines. The third group is a changeable figure. Can you see the differences in the arrangements of dots in the three groups? Do you understand why a changeable figure can be viewed in different ways?

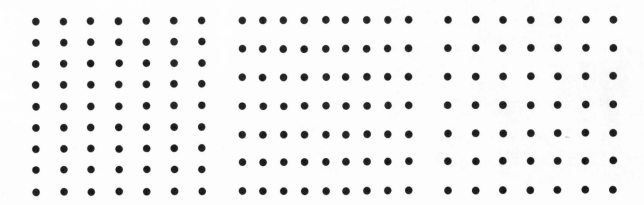

Figure 4–17

Depth and Distance

WIDE WORLD PHOTOS

Figure 5–1

Look at the photograph in Figure 5-1. Which of the cars seems farthest away? Which seems closest? Of course, this is an illusion. All the pictured cars are the same distance from you. The cars are as far away as the distance that you hold the book from your eyes.

You can easily understand why some cars seem more distant. Distant cars seem smaller to you than closer cars. If you watch a car moving toward you, it seems to get larger and larger. Very distant cars may look like dots. So how large something looks to you, helps you to tell how far away it is.

But size alone is not always enough to help you tell distance. Suppose you don't know the real size of the object. Then you may see an object as smaller either because it really *is* smaller or because it's farther away. In Figure 5-2, is box B smaller or more distant than box A?

Suppose we show box B as being a bit higher and add a few lines (Figure 5-3). Now how does it look?

When lines slant toward each other, you see them as being farther away. You can see the same effect in the drawing on page 41. The added lines help us to see the

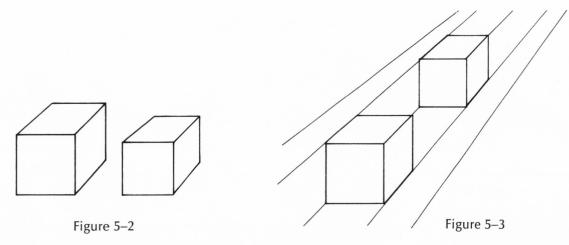

Figure 5–2

Figure 5–3

boxes in perspective. Lines that appear to come together in the distance are a powerful force in making you see illusions. For example, look at the drawing of a perfect square (Figure 5-4).

Because of the slanting lines, the top of the drawing seems farther away than the bottom. The slanting lines around the square seem to suggest that the top of the square is also farther away than the bottom. But the top and bottom of the square are the same size. So if the top is the same apparent size and yet farther away, it must be a little larger than the bottom. You can get rid of the illusion by getting rid of the surrounding lines. Use four index cards to cover the lines at the top, bottom, and sides of the square. Does it look like a square now?

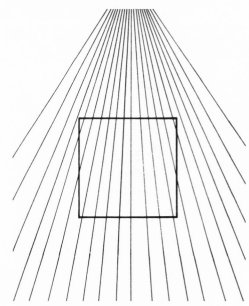

Figure 5–4

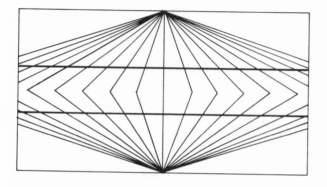

Figure 5–5

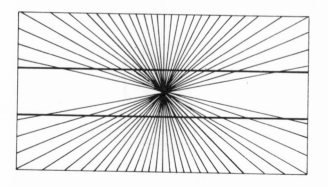

Figure 5–6

Here are some other illusions brought about by slanting lines that appear to vanish in the distance. Figure 5-5 seems to bulge toward you in the center and away from you at the sides, the top, and the bottom. The two horizontal lines are really parallel.

The same two parallel lines are in Figure 5-6. Now the slanting lines seem to meet in the distance in the center of the drawing. How do the parallel lines look different than in Figure 5-5?

Shading and shadow also helps you see distance or depth. Look at the two objects in Figure 5-7. One looks like a ball and the other looks like a flat circle. The ball seems to have a light shining on it from one side. The shadow and the difference in shading makes you see the object as a solid ball rather than as a circle.

A big help in finding out the shape or the distance of an object is to look at it with two eyes. Hold up a pencil. Close your left eye and look at the pencil with your right eye. Now look at the pencil with your left eye only. The two images are slightly different. When you look at the pencil with both eyes at the same time, the pencil looks solid.

Two photographs taken from the same distance apart as your eyes will look solid when viewed together. Perhaps you have seen some of these three dimensional photographs. You must use a special viewer to look at them. When you look into the viewer, your right eye looks at a slightly different photo than your left eye. Your brain puts both pictures together and gives you the illusion of looking at solid objects in three dimensions.

Here is a way to show that you see a scene at a slightly different angle with each eye. Hold a pencil about one foot in front of your eyes. Look at the room beyond the pencil. Close first one eye and then the other. Notice the way the pencil appears to move against the background. Of course, the pencil isn't moving. What's moving is your point of view.

Get a friend to help you with this next experience. You will also need two pencils. Hold a pencil in each hand. Have your friend stand across the room from you.

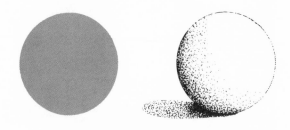

Figure 5–7

Tell your friend that you are going to start one pencil closer and then move it farther away from him. He is to tell you when the moving pencil seems the same distance from him as the stationary pencil.

First let him try to tell the distance of the pencils with both of his eyes open. Then let him try to tell with only one eye open. You'll be surprised at how much difference there will be when he views the pencils with one eye.

In spite of the fact that you use both eyes to see distance and depth, you use one of your eyes more than the other. Here's how to find out which one. Extend your arm and point your finger directly at a distant object. Now shut first one eye then the other. You'll find that you are pointing at the object with one eye but not with the other. The eye that you use for pointing is the one you use more.

Ask your friends to try the same experiment. You will find that some people use their right eye and some people use their left eye. It seems that just as some people are right-handed and others left-handed, some are right-eyed and others left-eyed.

You don't see a bright object in the same way as you see a dim object. A brightly lit white object produces an image on your retina that spreads out slightly. This makes it appear slightly larger than a dimly lit object of the same size. For example, look at Figure 6-1 in bright light. The white square appears larger than the black square even though they are of equal size.

In Figure 6-2, the white inner circle seems larger than the black inner circle. Again, they are really of equal size.

Everything looks larger if it reflects more light. A fat person looks thinner in dark clothing than in light clothing. A brightly colored box of cornflakes seems larger than a darkly colored box. The filament of a light bulb in a flashlight appears larger when it is giving off light.

Here's how to do an experiment that shows this effect. You will need a candle, matches, and a ruler. *Caution: Perform this experiment with care.* Light the candle. Hold the ruler in front of the flame so that only the top part of the flame is visible. The ruler will appear to be notched where the bright light of the flame seems to spread out.

The background against which we see an object has

Brightness and Contrast

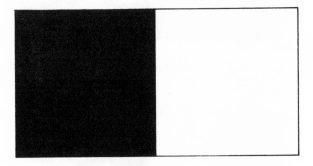

Figure 6–1

Figure 6–2

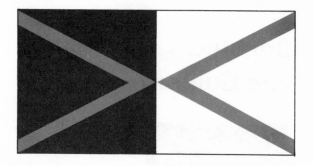

Figure 6–3

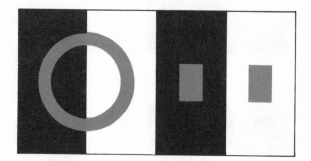

Figure 6–4

a great influence on what we see. Figure 6-3 shows stripes of gray that are exactly the same shade. Yet the gray on the white background looks much darker than the gray on the dark background.

Figure 6-4 shows some gray circles and some gray boxes that are all the same shade. How do they look to you?

If the contrast between a bright and a dim object is too great, you will not be able to even see the dim object. On the road at night, you can't see a car behind a headlight when the headlight is shining in your eyes.

Figure 6–5

When your room is brightly lit at night, someone can see in through the window glass but you can't see out through it.

Here's a funny effect that you get from brightness contrast. Look at Figure 6-5. Do you see gray dots at the intersections of the white lines. If you stare at one of the dots, it may go away, but the dots around it will appear darker.

In Figure 6-6, you can see white dots where the black lines intersect. Again, if you stare at one of the dots it will disappear.

Figure 6–6

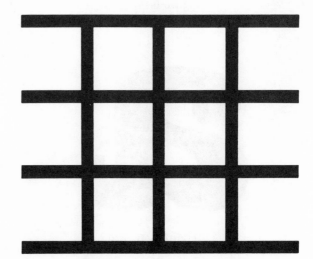

Figure 6–7

Figure 6–8

The ghostly dots that you see at the intersections may have something to do with your retina getting tired of staring at an object. Retinal fatigue can give you something called an afterimage. Look at the white crosses in Figure 6-7 under a bright light. Stare at them a few minutes without shifting your eyes. Then look at a sheet of blank white paper. What do you see?

Even the black print of the book that you are reading is part of an illusion. It looks darker than it really is because of the white paper on which it is printed. Look at the large letter in Figure 6-8. Make a small hole in a piece of black velvet cloth. Lay the hole over part of the letter. Does the print look as dark when it is surrounded by black as it does when it is surrounded by white?

Your eye contains two different kinds of nerve cells: rods and cones. These two types of cells have different jobs. The cones give us the ability to see colors. The rods are sensitive to shades of brightness. We use the cones more during the day and in bright light. We use the rods more at night and when the light is dim.

In the center of the retina (see page 13) are many cones and no rods. Around the outer edges of the retina, the number of cones decrease while there are more and more rods.

The tiny spot in the center of your eye that contains only cones is where you get the sharpest image. If you glimpse something out of the corner of your eye that you want to see more clearly, you turn your eye so that the image of the object falls onto the central spot.

Here's how you can show that the central spot of your retina is not very sensitive to dim light. Go out-of-doors on a clear night and look up at the starry sky. Pick out one medium bright star. Now stare directly at it without shifting your eyes. The star will dim and almost disappear because of the absence of light-sensitive rods in the

Color

center spot. But if you glance a little to the side, the star will suddenly brighten. That's because the star's image is falling on the rods around the edges of your retina.

The lack of bright light at night is the reason why everything looks gray. Sunlight is about 160,000 times as bright as moonlight. The silvery light of the moon is the result of your viewing it with color-blind rods. The color-sensing cones do not respond to the moon's dim light.

Of course, your eyes alone do not see color. Like every other kind of visual experience, your brain plays an important role in the colors you see.

You can show how your brain is involved in sensing colors with a device called a color wheel. Cut out a circle of white cardboard about four inches in diameter. Color half the circle bluish-green and the other half red. Push a pin through the center of the cardboard disc. Hold the disc in the sunlight or under a very bright light and then spin it as rapidly as you can.

The bright colors will combine with each other and you will see a neutral or grayish tint. You can show the same thing by coloring one half of the disc greenish-yellow and the other half violet. Using a hand drill to spin the disc faster makes the demonstration work even better.

Here's more evidence of the role your brain plays in seeing color: You will need a piece of red cellophane and a piece of green cellophane. Hold the red cellophane in front of one eye and the green cellophane in front of the other eye. Now look at a sheet of white paper. You might be surprised at the result. The two color sensations are combined in your brain. You see a sheet of white paper without any trace of the red or the green.

The colors you see are influenced by the surroundings. Construct a star on a piece of white paper as in Figure 7-1.

Color the star with an orange marker. Look at the star in dim light and then in bright light. How does the orange appear to change?

If you have different colored bulbs such as those on a string of Christmas tree lights, look at the star in blue or green light and then in yellow or red light. The star looks

Figure 7–1

much more intensely orange in the contrasting blue or green light than in the more similar yellow or red light.

Colors affect each other when you see them together. You can demonstrate this by drawing and coloring the same color orange star on several sheets of paper. Color the background differently in each case. Which colors seem to have the greatest effect on the orange? Which seem to have the least effect?

Now look at an orange star through a small hole in a piece of white cardboard. It will look different in color and brightness than when you view it against its colored surroundings.

Another interesting color illusion that you can demonstrate is called an afterimage. After staring at a bright object for a time and then looking away, you will see an afterimage of the same shape and size but of a different color.

Try this. Use a bright red magic marker to color a square on a sheet of white paper. Hold the paper under a bright light and stare steadily for thirty seconds at the center of the red square. Still keeping your eyes fixed at the same spot, replace the paper with a sheet of blank white paper. Keep staring at the blank paper and in a few seconds you'll see the square reappear. Only this time the square will be green rather than red.

You are seeing an afterimage of the red square. If you shift your eyes and look around the blank paper, the afterimage will fade away. It will last longer when you stare at the original image for a longer time in bright light.

If you try the same experiment but start out with a green square, the afterimage will be red or pink. Other color combinations you will get with afterimages are blue with orange and yellow with violet. These color-pairs are called complementary colors. When the lights of complementary color-pairs are mixed together, the result is white light.

All lights have color, even white light. White light is really the sum of certain colored lights. Red, green, and blue light mixed together add up to white light. But these three colored lights when mixed in different amounts can also produce any other color. Scientists call them the primary colors of light.

Opposite each primary color is its complementary color. For example cyan (a kind of bluish-green) is the complement of red; yellow is the complement of blue; and magenta (a kind of purple) is the complement of green. Colors in between these primaries and their complements have their own complements. Scientists and artists often use a color wheel with all the colors in a circle. From this wheel the complementary colors can easily be identified. Complementary colors are opposite one another on the wheel.

When you stare at one of a pair of complementary colors, your eyes seem to become fatigued with that color. For example, when you stare at a red square, your eyes tire of red. When you switch over to looking at a white surface, your eyes subtract the red you were staring at and you see its complementary color, green.

You can use your knowledge of afterimages to construct some amusing posters to show your family and friends. For example, you can draw an American flag on a large white poster. But this American flag is unlike any you have ever seen. Use magic markers to make seven green stripes alternating with six black stripes. Color the stars black against an orange field.

Now hang the flag on a wall. Hang a blank white poster nearby. Shine a bright light on the peculiar flag and ask your friends to stare directly at it for thirty seconds. Now have your friends look at the blank poster. Lo and behold. They will see an afterimage of the American flag in its true colors—red, white, and blue.

Other drawings you can make for their afterimages include a purple cow, violet bananas, a green-suited Santa Claus with a black beard, and a green sunset. Experiment to see which afterimages other colors produce. Perhaps you can prepare an afterimage show for your friends and classmates.

Optical Illusions in Art

Painters and other artists have used optical illusions since the early beginnings of art. As far back as prehistoric cave drawings, artists have tried to show the real, three-dimensional world on a flat two-dimensional surface. Perspective, light and shade, contrast, and color are some of the tools that artists use to achieve their effects.

It is interesting to look at drawings or paintings and try to pick out the ways in which the artist uses his materials to make you see with the artist's own vision. For example, look at the print of a landscape by the seventeenth-century artist Jacob van Ruisdael (Figure 8-1).

Can you tell the materials which were used in the construction of the cottage? How does the artist set the mood of the day? Notice the use of shading and line to show the difference between water and land. Despite the many years that have passed since the print was made, the scene is a familiar one that we recognize quickly.

But look at the print made by the eighteenth-century artist Piranesi (Figure 8-2). The title of the print is *Prisons,*

Figure 8–1   VAN RUISDAEL, JACOB
Luogo roccioso
Alinari/Art Resource, Inc.

but no prisons such as these ever existed outside the artist's mind.

The artist makes you see huge and deep spaces with stone arches, timbers, and ropes. He uses perspective, light and shade, and contrasting shades of gray. Bridges and stairs seem to go no place and have no reason. You see a solid structure made of huge blocks of stone. Yet it is somehow unreal and shadowy.

Figure 8–2
PIRANESI, GIOVANNI BATTISTA
Carceri d'Invenzione
Alinari/Art Resource, Inc.

Figure 8–3

ESCHER, M.C.
Day and Night
© Beeldrecht,
Amsterdam/VAGA, New
York Collection Haags
Gemeentemuseum—The
Hague

Modern artists have gone even further with the use of optical illusions. One of the most interesting uses of different kinds of illusions is found in the works of the twentieth-century artist M. C. Escher. Figure 8-3 is a work of his called *Day and Night.*

Look carefully at the picture and describe what you see. Do you see the white birds flying off to the right and the black birds flying to the left? Look how the birds merge into sections of the landscape. In the center of the print, each bird is outlined by the shapes of other birds. As you look, your perceptions change.

Figure 8-4 is a print by Escher called *Another World.* The scene is startling. Not only does it show a weird figure against a strange background, but directions and distances are confused and meaningless. Which way is up or down? From what angle are you looking at the picture?

Escher uses optical illusions to make you believe in impossible places. In a small area on a flat surface, Escher shows you the mind-spinning strangeness of distant universes.

Figure 8-5 is another print by Escher that may remind you in certain ways of the Piranesi *Prisons.*

Stairs go up and down. But where do they lead? Who are the figures and what are they doing? It all depends on your point of view. When the great scientist Einstein

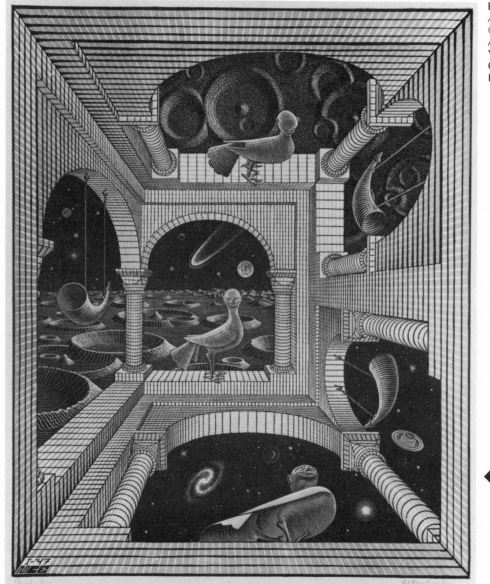

◀ Figure 8–4

Figure 8–5 ▶

Figure 8–6
ESCHER, M.C.
Waterfall
© Beeldrecht, Amsterdam/VAGA, New York
Collection Haags Gemeentemuseum—The Hague

Figure 8–7

VASARELY, VICTOR
Ondho 1956-60
Oil on Canvas, 7′ 2⅝″ x 71″
Collection, The Museum of Modern Art,
New York
Gift of G. David Thompson

developed his theory of relativity, it made scientists see and understand in new ways. Escher tries to make us see in new ways with his own "relativity."

Look at Figure 8-6. Follow the path of the waterfall all around the building. Do you believe what you see? How can water keep flowing around and around and

Figure 8–8
ALBERS, JOSEF
White Embossings on Gray VIII
Personal Collection of Kenneth E. Tyler

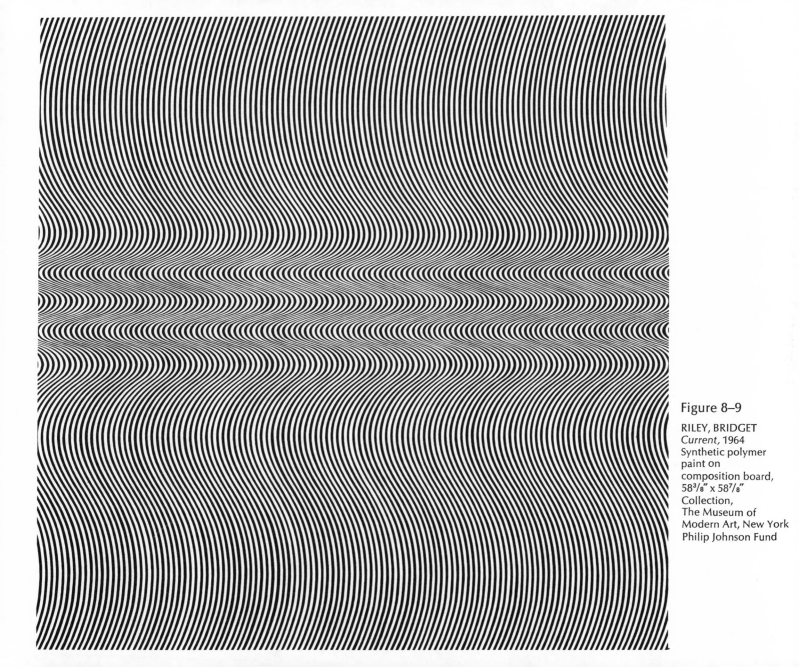

yet downhill all the time? The illusion is so convincing that you'll have a hard time figuring out why you see it. One clue is to check the columns as they support each level.

There are many other artists who use optical illusions in important ways in their works. Figure 8-7 is a print of a painting called *Ondho* by the contemporary artist Victor Vasarely. Changes in the size and the shape of the squares and circles and the position of the lines make the figures appear to advance and retreat in our eyes.

Another contemporary artist who uses illusions is Josef Albers. Look at his *White Embossings on Gray VIII* (Figure 8-8). Are you sure you see them the way you think you do? Look again.

Finally, Figure 8-9 is an example of a form of art called optical or op-art. It is by the contemporary artist Bridget Riley. The title is *Current*. No matter how still you keep your eyes, the picture seems to be in motion.

There are lots of optical illusions that you can try out by yourself or with your friends. Here's a sampling of some that are fun.

You can make a cartoon character move very much the way they do in the movies. You will need a few sheets of typing paper, a pair of scissors, a stapler or a large paper clip, and a pen or pencil. Cut the paper into strips about 1½ inches wide by 3 inches long. You will need about thirty or forty strips. Stack them neatly and staple or clip them together along the bottom. Now draw a picture on each one of the strips that is just a little bit different than the one before it. For example, you might have a figure running or a rocket ship moving across the page as shown in Figure 9-1. Now hold the bottom of the stack firmly with your left hand. With your right hand, bend the strips backward and allow them to flip forward. You will get an illusion of motion. The rocket ship will appear to move or the figure will appear to run across the strips.

More Optical Illusions to Try

Figure 9–1

Figure 9–2

This uses the same principle as do regular movies. Your eyes keep an image for a short time. If you see another image in quick succession, your eyes blend the images together and you see the illusion of motion. In the movies, still pictures are projected on the screen at the rate of twenty-four every second. Each still picture is slightly different than the one before just as in your book. You will see these still pictures with the illusion of movement.

The word *moiré* is used to describe the patterns you get when you overlap two or more similar patterns that have regular spacing. All you need to make a moiré is two metal screens or two wide-meshed nylon stockings. Hold the screens or stockings one in front of another. Turn them in different directions. As you turn them against each other, you will see changing moiré patterns develop. The explanation for your seeing a moiré pattern is quite complicated. But what seems to be important is the way you see the points where one line intersects another. Any kind of regular patterns superimposed atop one another will produce a moiré. Look at Figure 9-2.

Look at the spiral in Figure 9-3. Now revolve it around. When you revolve the spiral in one direction, the lines seem to move toward the center. When you revolve it in the other direction, the lines seem to move outward from the center. Perhaps you have seen a toy that works on the same principle. When you spin the toy, the spiral on it seems to become smaller or larger depending on the direction of the spin.

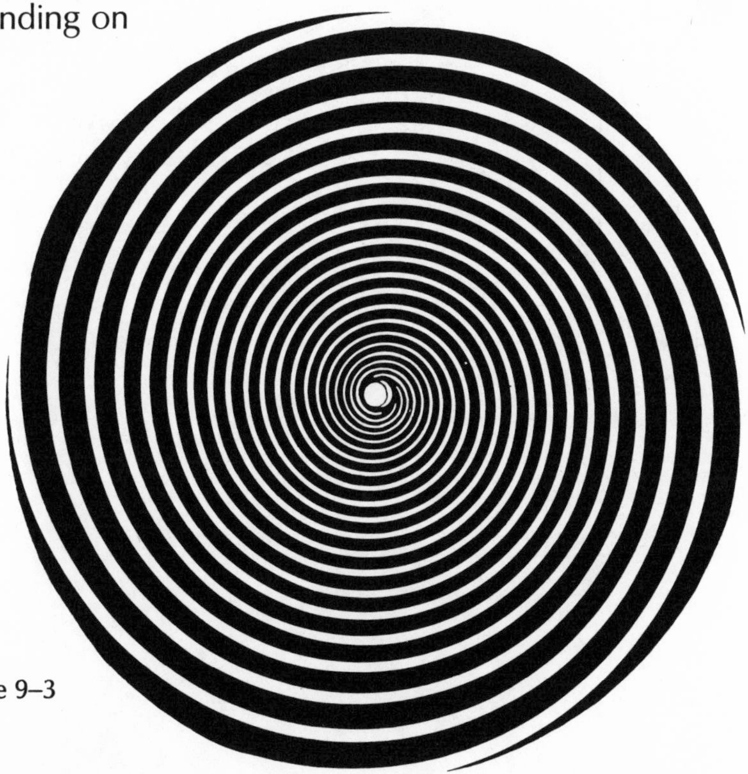

Figure 9–3

Remember the impossible figure on page 11? Figure 9-4 is an impossible triangle. Each angle is reasonable, but all the angles placed together are impossible. The reason it looks that way is that it is really a flat drawing, not a three dimensional object. But we see it in three dimensions in an impossible way.

Draw a perfect square with exactly equal sides. Does it look perfect? Now draw a square a bit shorter than it is wide. Look at it side by side with the perfect square (Figure 9-5). You'll find that the unequal-sided square (A) looks more equal than the perfect square (B).

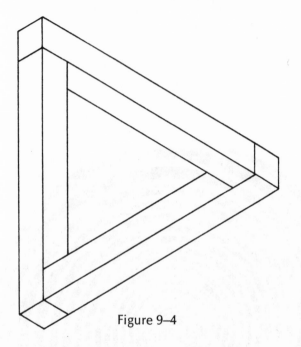

Figure 9–4

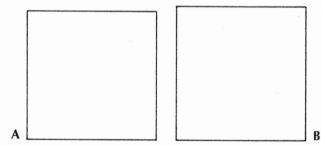

Figure 9–5

One of the most common optical illusions in nature is called a mirage. You may have seen a mirage while walking or riding down a street on a hot day. Down the way you suddenly see what looks like a pool of water on the pavement. But the pool is an illusion. It keeps retreating from you as you try to reach it.

The mirage is due to changes in the atmosphere just above the surface of the ground. The ground gets very hot under a summer sun and heats the air right above it. The rising air causes changes in the direction of light rays passing through. You see these changes as ripples and movements that look like water.

These changes in the atmosphere account for the mirages of lakes in the desert and icebergs in the sea. But any more complicated mirages, such as an ice cream soda or a bathtub filled with ice water, are probably just the result of an overactive imagination.

Optical illusions are interesting and fun. Ask your family, friends, and classmates to tell what they see in an illusion. Perhaps they can suggest other illusions you can try out. You might keep a notebook containing descriptions of the optical illusions you tried and your results. Then anytime you like you can see again the ones you enjoyed the most.

INDEX

Escher, M. C., 58–64
eyes
  basic functioning of, 12–16
  central spot of, giving sharpest image, 49–50
  and color perception, 50
  dominant eye, 44
  viewing with one eye, 42–44

illusions. *See* optical illusions
imagination, and perception of illusions, 35–36
iris, 12

lens, of eye, 12–13
light
  as artist's tool, 56–57
  change in direction of rays of, 71
  and color perception, 49–53
  how focused on the eye, 12–13, 15

and perception of size, 45
primary colors of, 53
white, 53
See also brightness

mirage, 71
moiré, 68
motion, illusion of, 66–68, 71
movies, 67–68
Muller-Lyer illusion, 20–22

nature, optical illusions in, 9, 71
nerve cells
  in brain, 12, 14
  cones, 13, 49
  electrical currents from. *See* nerve impulses
  in eye, 12–13, 15
  in optic nerve, 12, 14
  rods, 13, 49
nerve impulses, 13–15

Ondho, 66
op-art. *See* optical art
optical art, 66
optical illusions
   in art, 9–10, 18–19, 56–66
   that change back and forth, 31–39. *See also* point
     of view
   cultural differences in perception of, 19–22
   defined, 9
   of movement, 66–68, 71
   in nature, 9, 71
   of size, 19, 45. *See also* perspective
   theories to explain, 17–22
optic nerve, 12, 14–15

perspective, 18–25, 41, 56–57
photographs, 22
   and perspective, 19–20
   three-dimensional, 43
Piranesi, 56–57, 59
point of view, 24, 43. *See also* changeable figures

previous-experience theory, 19–22
primary colors, 53–54
Prisons, 56–57, 59
pupil, of eye, 12

retina
   blind spot on, 15–16
   and color vision, 49–50
   fatigue of, 48
   function of, 12–15, 45
   See also cones; rods
retinal fatigue, 48
reversing cube, 31
Riley, Bridget, 66
rods, 13, 15, 49–50
   color-blindness of, 50
   sensitivity to brightness, 49–50
Ruisdael, Jacob van, 56

shading, 42, 56–57
shape, three-dimensional, 42–43